PRAYERS
TO OUR LADY
EAST AND WEST

ORTHODOX LOGOS PUBLISHING

PRAYERS TO OUR LADY EAST AND WEST

by Deacon David Lochbihler, J.D.

Cover photo by Subdeacon Alex Taylor

Book cover and layout by Max Mendor

Publishers Maxim Hodak & Max Mendor

© 2021, Orthodox Logos Publishing,

The Netherlands

www.orthodoxlogos.com

ISBN: 978-1-914337-11-6
ISBN: 978-1-914337-05-5
ISBN: 978-1-80484-046-7

This book is in copyright. No part of this publication may be reproduced, stored in a retrieval system or transmitted in any form or by any means without the prior permission in writing of the publisher, nor be otherwise circulated in any form of binding or cover other than that in which it is published without a similar condition, including this condition, being imposed on the subsequent purchaser.

DEACON DAVID LOCHBIHLER, J.D.

PRAYERS
TO OUR LADY
EAST AND WEST

ORTHODOX LOGOS PUBLISHING

CONTENTS

ACKNOWLEDGEMENTS 9

INTRODUCTION 11

THE PRAYER RULE
OF THE THEOTOKOS 17

THE ROSARY 29

THEOLOGICAL REFLECTION 40

CONCLUSION 48

BIBLIOGRAPHY 52

To Lindsay Marie, Patrick, & Maggie

ACKNOWLEDGEMENTS

This book was written while earning a Master's Degree in Applied Orthodox Theology from the University of Balamand in Lebanon at the Antiochian House of Studies in North America. I want to thank Metropolitan Joseph of the Antiochian Archdiocese of North America for approving my ordination to the diaconate at the Western Rite Conference in Fort Worth, Texas, last year, Bishop John for ordaining me at Saint Patrick Orthodox Church on Saint Patrick's Day 2019, and Bishop Thomas for being such a special friend to our Saint Patrick community, never missing our special Feast Day.

    The wonder-full people of Saint Patrick Orthodox Church are simply the best. Father Patrick and Khouria Kerrie Cardine and their six delightful children always welcome me into their home as have friends Drew and Cecelia Dohm. Deacon Douglas and Shamassy Phyllis King guided me into the diaconate. Prior to becoming a Deacon, I served for more than five years as a Subdeacon, and it has been an honour to serve alongside Subdeacons Steve, Jim, Scott, Anthony, Alex, and John Wiley. It is a joy to lead the Altar Servers and teach Sunday School at Saint Patrick Orthodox Church.

Special thanks also to David and Jo Thoburn, Rosemary Thoburn, and my students, players, parents, and colleagues at The Fairfax Christian School in Dulles, Virginia, where I teach 4th Grade and coach varsity high school basketball. Working with fine colleagues like David McElfresh, Coleene Wilhelm, and Eric Duncanson is a joy.

I am extremely grateful to my thesis advisor Father Edward Hughes for his holy friendship and prayerful guidance in completing this work. I also want to thank Metropolitan Kallistos Ware, Father Peter Gillquist of blessed memory, his wife Khouria Marilyn, Father Alexander Atty of blessed memory, Father Patrick Cardine, Father Anthony Messeh, and Father Tom Palke for guiding me into Orthodoxy.

Finally, a heartfelt thank you to Maxim Hodak, Max Mendor, and Orthodox Logos in the Netherlands for publishing this book. Your commitment to excellence in promoting the Orthodox Faith is a most essential gift to the world.

Every single error in this book is entirely my own. I would love to hear from you, my beloved reader, if any small part of this work touches your heart.

> Friends in Jesus and Mary,
> Deacon David Lochbihler
> Saint Patrick Orthodox Church
> The Nativity of the Blessed Virgin Mary
> Sunday 8 September 2019
> orthodoxdeacondavid@gmail.com

INTRODUCTION

"More honourable than the Cherubim, and beyond compare more glorious than the Seraphim, thee who without corruption gavest birth to God the Word, the very Theotokos, thee do we magnify."[1] These words of veneration for the Blessed Virgin Mary, prayed and sung throughout the Orthodox Church for centuries, epitomize the special love relationship between the Theotokos and the Orthodox faithful.

"Throughout history, and especially during the fourth and fifth centuries, the basic category for thinking about Mary was that of paradox: Virgin and Mother; Human Mother of One who is God, Theotokos."[2] A theological understanding of Our Lady is found most readily in the Divine Liturgy. "In Orthodox services Mary is often mentioned, and on each occasion she is usually given her full title: 'Our All-Holy, immaculate, most blessed and glorified Lady, Mother of God and Ever-Virgin Mary.' Here are included the three chief epithets applied to Our Lady by

---

[1] Holy Transfiguration Monastery, trans., *The Service of the Akathist Hymn: The Salutations to the Most Holy Theotokos*, (Boston, MA: Holy Transfiguration Monastery, 1991), 79.

[2] Jaroslav Pelikan, *Mary Through the Centuries* (New Haven and London: Yale University Press, 1996), 55.

the Orthodox Church: *Theotokos* (God-bearer, Mother of God), *Aeiparthenos* (Ever-Virgin), and *Panagia* (All-Holy-)."[3] The veracity of these titles for the Blessed Virgin Mary has been affirmed throughout church history, especially in the ecumenical councils. "The authority for these epithets is to be found in the records of the early ecumenical councils."[4] The veneration of Our Lady permeates the life of the Orthodox Church. "Although these titles have never been defined explicitly in an ecumenical council of the Eastern Orthodox Churches, they are used frequently in liturgy and personal prayer."[5] Every Orthodox Church features an icon of the Virgin Mary and the Child Jesus near the altar, and our people's intense love for the Theotokos runs wide and deep. These three titles of the Virgin Mary will be considered in turn.

The Virgin Mary is called the Theotokos or God-bearer from the earliest centuries of the Orthodox faith. Around the year 250 A.D., the term *Theotokos* "was found in a prayer written on a fragment of Egyptian papyrus for use during the Coptic Nativity Liturgy. The prayer is known as the *Sub Tuum Praesidium* (translated into English as, "Beneath Thy Compassion"). The significance of the use

....

[3] Timothy Ware, *The Orthodox Church* (London: Penguin Books, 1997), 257-258.

[4] Andrew Louth, "John of Damascus on the Mother of God as a Link Between Humanity and God," Chap. 10 in *The Cult of the Mother of God in Byzantium,* ed. Leslie Brubaker and Mary Cunningham (Burlington, VT: Ashgate Publishing, 2011), 154.

[5] Mary Christine Athans, *In Quest of the Jewish Mary* (Maryknoll, NY: Orbis Books, 2013), 27.

of this written word in this prayer indicates that it was in common use during this liturgy and most likely used at least decades prior."[6] In addition, as most likely the oral tradition precedes the written word, it is likely the figure of the Virgin Mary was venerated quite early in church history. "Precisely because the Son of God became incarnate in Mary's womb, she is rightly called Mother of God."[7]

Mary also is referred to as *Aeiparthenos*, the Ever-Virgin. "Turning to the Fathers, one of the first proclamations of the doctrine of the virginal conception is by Ignatius of Antioch,"[8] a saint and bishop living in the first and second centuries. Saint Ambrose (340-397) "appreciated how hard it was to maintain Christian virginity, and so he offered Mary as a companion to the celibates who tried. The purity of her body and her decorous comportment were to be emulated by women who strove for virtue, since Mary was a mirror of all virtues."[9] Mary as Ever-Virgin cleanses those mired in sin and striving for holiness: "O Pure One without flaw, Holy One without blemish, Cleanse me that I might become pure. Sanctify me and I shall be made

---

[6] Andrew Gary Podolak, "*Most Holy Theotokos, Save Us*," Master's thesis, Balamand University, 2015, 12.

[7] Luigi Gambero, *Mary and the Fathers of the Church: The Blessed Virgin Mary in Patristic Thought* (San Francisco: Ignatius Press, 1999), 153.

[8] Brian K. Reynolds, *Gateway to Heaven: Marian Doctrine and Devotion Image and Typology in the Patristic and Medieval Period*, vol. 1 (Hyde Park, NY: New City Press, 2012), 54.

[9] Miri Rubin, *Mother of God: A History of the Virgin Mary* (New Haven & London: Yale University Press, 2009), 27.

holy."[10] The Virgin Mary inspires all Orthodox Christians, both celibate and married, to live purer and more chaste lives faithful to their calling. "Blessed is she who received the Holy Spirit; He purified and polished her, and He made her a temple, and the Lord Most High dwelt in her abode."[11] Mary's virginity makes her uniqueness as the Mother of God even more pronounced, as only a pure and holy woman would be able to bear the Son of God in her virginal womb.

Besides being the Mother of God and pure virgin, Mary is called *Panagia*, the All-Holy. "Mary became 'all holy' as a result of the process of *theosis* (deification or divinization), and this was the result of both 'her free will and consent and … of the grace of the Logos of God.'"[12] After Mary assents to become the Mother of Jesus, the Holy Spirit "sanctified her, purified her and made her blessed among women… She was summoned that she might be the Mother of the Son of God; the Holy Spirit had sanctified her and so dwelt within her."[13] How was Mary, born of a man and a woman, able to overcome the corruption of the human propensity to sin? "The Son of

---

[10] John Anthony McGuckin, *The Harp of Glory: Enzira Sebhat* (Yonkers, NY: St. Vladimir's Seminary Press, 2010), 63.

[11] Jacob of Serug, *On the Mother of God* (Crestwood, NY: St. Vladimir's Seminary Press, 1998), 41.

[12] Robert L. Fastiggi, "The Immaculate Conception: Historical and Ecumenical Perspectives," in *De Maria Numquam Satis: The Significance of the Catholic Doctrines on the Blessed Virgin Mary*, ed. Judith Marie Gentle and Robert L. Fastiggi, 1-16. Lanham, MD: University Press of America, 2009, 9.

[13] Jacob of Serug, *On the Mother of God*, 34.

God wanted to be related to her, and first He made her body without sin."[14] The glorification of Mary resounds from the angelic hosts in heaven: "The heavenly company performed their 'Holy, Holy, Holy,' unto the glorious soul of this Mother of the Son of God."[15]

Saint Ambrose "places his Mariology firmly within the Christological context."[16] Specifically, for Saint Ambrose, "the Virgin Birth is closely related to the divinity of Christ."[17] Mary's status within the Orthodox Church exists primarily because of her pivotal role in the mystery of the Incarnation. "Anyone who thinks out the implications of that great phrase, *The Word was made flesh*, cannot but feel a profound awe for her who was chosen as the instrument of so surpassing a mystery."[18] The essence of the Incarnation is remembered and recited at the end of every Western Rite Mass, as the priest reads about the Incarnation of Jesus from John 1:1-18 in the Last Gospel after the Final Blessing of the people. In addition, just prior to the singing of the closing recessional hymn, the priest and people pray the Angelus together. The Theotokos is immersed in the mystery of the Incarnation, next to the Trinity the most profound mystery of our faith. "She gave flesh to her Son, and she is this God-bearing and theoph-

---

[14] Ibid., 35.

[15] Ibid., 98.

[16] Hilda Graef, *Mary: A History of Doctrine and Devotion*, vol. 1 (New York: Sheed and Ward, 1963), 78.

[17] Ibid., 79.

[18] Ware, *The Orthodox Church*, 258.

oric flesh through which the flesh of the world is brought to Him for salvation."[19] Her unique role in the Incarnation is both essential and indispensable.

This book will compare and contrast two devotional prayers venerating the Theotokos, the Blessed Virgin Mary: *The Prayer Rule of the Theotokos* and the Rosary. At the heart of each prayer, a special tribute to Our Lady is spoken most often. First, from *The Prayer Rule of the Theotokos*, the following prayer to the Theotokos is said: "Rejoice, O Virgin Theotokos Mary, full of grace, the Lord is with You. Blessed are you among women, and blessed is the fruit of Your womb, for you have born Christ, the Savior of our souls."[20] Second, the "centerpiece of the Rosary"[21] is the Hail Mary: "Hail Mary, full of grace. The Lord is with thee. Blessed art thou among women, and blessed is the fruit of thy womb, Jesus. Holy Mary, Mother of God, pray for us sinners, now and at the hour of our death. Amen."[22] The history and devotion underlining these two prayers within the context of the Western Rite Rosary will be considered in turn.

---

[19] Sergius Bulgakov, *The Burning Bush: On the Orthodox Veneration of the Mother of God* (Grand Rapids, MI: William B. Eerdsman Publishing, 2009), 111.

[20] Anthony Stehlin, *The Prayer Rule of the Theotokos as Prayed by Saint Seraphim of Sarov* (Middletown, DE: Chi Rho Publishing, 2015), iv.

[21] Patricia Ann Kasten, *Lining Your Beads: The Rosaries History, Mysteries, and Prayers* (Huntington, IN: Our Sunday Visitor, 2010), 48.

[22] Ibid., 52-53.

THE PRAYER RULE OF THE THEOTOKOS

"Rejoice, O Virgin Theotokos Mary, full of grace, the Lord is with You. Blessed are you among women, and blessed is the fruit of Your womb, for you have born Christ, the Savior of our souls."[23]

"The first and greatest of the *startsy* of the nineteenth century was St Seraphim of Sarov (1759-1833)."[24] He entered the monastery at the age of nineteen, lived in the community for sixteen years, and then withdrew to spend the next two decades of his life in seclusion.[25] As the elder of the Sarov Monastery, Seraphim loved and served the people. "From dawn until evening he received all who came to him for help, healing the sick, giving advice, often supplying the answer before his visitor had time to ask any questions. Sometimes scores or hundreds would come to see him in a single day."[26] While Seraphim ministered

---

[23] Stehlin, *The Prayer Rule of the Theotokos as Prayed by Saint Seraphim of Sarov*, iv.

[24] Ware, *The Orthodox Church*, 118.

[25] Ibid.

[26] Ibid.

during his life at the Sarov Monastery, nearby the sisters lived in the Diveyevo Convent. It is within the context of Saint Seraphim's reflections upon the Diveyevo Convent that we learn of *The Prayer Rule of the Theotokos*.

Ivan Mikhailovich Andreyevsky (1894-1976), with the literary pseudonym of Andreyev, describes a most memorable visit to the Diveyevo Convent. "It was the custom for pilgrims to Diveyevo to remain at least 24 hours in the Convent and perform there the 'rule' laid down by St. Seraphim himself: to walk three times around the 'canal' of the Mother of God (the path around the Convent), saying a special rule of prayer by prayer-rope, praying for all one's relations and close ones, and at the end expressing one's most heartfelt, most needed desire, which would unfailingly be granted, according to one's prayer."[27] Andreyev completed this pilgrimage, concluding with this heartfelt prayer: "O Lord, give me nothing, *take away* from me all earthly prosperity, but only do not deprive me of the joy of communion with Thee, or, if it is impossible to preserve this always in our life, then grant me remembrance of heart, grant me the possibility of preserving to death the remembrance of this present blessed minute of the sensing of Thy Holy Spirit."[28] During this prayerful pilgrimage, Andreyev followed the spiritual guidance laid down in the past by Saint Seraphim of Sarov, and this rule

---

[27] "I. M. Andreyev: True Orthodox Convert from the Russian Intelligentsia," *The Orthodox Word 73*, 13.2, (March-April 1977), 62.
[28] Ibid., 63.

prescribed by the great saint indeed may be *The Prayer Rule of the Theotokos.*

Like Saint Seraphim of Sarov, Father Zachariah, given the name of Father Zosima in the monastery, was a nineteenth century *startsy*. "Father Zosima had a special love for the Queen of Heaven. He seemed to be always standing before her."[29] His relationship with Our Lady was exceptionally personal and profound. "When the elder turned to the Queen of Heaven in prayer, he spoke to her as though she were alive and could see her right there in his cell. And in fact, the Queen of Heaven was always with him, and the entire inner and outward life of the elder passed under her protection."[30] Father Zosima "exhorted all his spiritual children to say daily, every hour of the twenty-four: 'Hail, Mother of God and Virgin, Mary full of grace, the Lord is with thee. Blessed art thou among women and blessed is the fruit of thy womb, for thou hast given birth to the Saviour of our souls.' (Translator's note.)"[31]

Just as Andreyev made the pilgrimage around the Diveyevo Convent, so too does Father Zosima describe in detail how Saint Seraphim encouraged his followers to pray *The Prayer Rule of the Theotokos* "along the ditch which encircled the Convent of Diveevo"[32] Father Alexan-

---

[29] Jane Ellis, trans., *An Early Soviet Saint: The Life of Father Zachariah* (London and Oxford: Mowbrays, 1976), 65.

[30] Ibid.

[31] Ibid.

[32] Ibid., 66.

der Gumanovsky, a spiritual son of Father Zosima, offered this advice: "Say the 'O Hail, Mother of God and Virgin' one hundred and fifty times, and this prayer will save you."[33] Father Alexander continues, "This Rule was given by the Mother of God herself in about the eighth century, and at one time all Christians fulfilled it."[34]

Although there exists no proof substantiating the eighth century origin of *The Prayer Rule of the Theotokos*, this Rule as practiced and prayed by Saint Seraphim, Father Zosima, and Father Alexander parallels the Western Rite Rosary. "If, being unaccustomed to it, it is difficult to master one hundred and fifty repetitions daily, say it fifty times at first. After every ten repetitions say the 'Our Father' once and 'Open unto us the door of thy loving-kindness, O blessed Mother of God; in that we set our hope on thee, we may not go astray; but through thee may we be delivered from all adversities, for thou art the salvation of all Christian people' (Translator's note)."[35]

Father Zosima also held Bishop Seraphim Zvezdinsky in high esteem, referring to him "as 'that saintly Bishop.'" Bishop Seraphim Zvezdinsky performed the Rule of the Mother of God every day, and when he performed it he prayed for the whole world, embracing in this rule the whole life of the Queen of Heaven.[36] Specifically, Bishop Seraphim developed a plan recalling and remembering

....

[33] Ibid., 67.
[34] Ibid.
[35] Ibid.
[36] Ibid.

fifteen key events in the life of Mary corresponding to the fifteen decades of *The Prayer Rule of the Theotokos*.

A very recent rendition of *The Prayer Rule of the Theotokos* is described as being prayed "by the great 19th Century Russian Orthodox Mystic, Saint Seraphim Of Sarov."[37] The preparatory prayers include:

1. (The Sign of the Cross): "In the Name of the Father, and of The Son, and of the Holy Spirit. Amen."[38]

2. "O God, be merciful to me a sinner. Glory to You, Our God, Glory to You! O Heavenly King, Comforter, Spirit of Truth, Everywhere present and filling all things, Treasury of blessings and Giver of Life: Come and dwell within us, cleanse us of all Stain, and save our souls, O gracious One."[39]

3. "Holy God, Holy Mighty, Holy Immortal, have mercy on us! Holy God, Holy Mighty, Holy Immortal, have mercy on us! Holy God, Holy Mighty, Holy Immortal, have mercy on us! Glory to the Father, and to the Son, and to the Holy Spirit, Now and ever and forever. Amen.
O Most Holy Trinity, have mercy on us. O Lord, cleanse Us of our sins. O Master forgive us our transgressions.
O Holy One, come to us and heal our infirmities,
For Your Name's sake."[40]

---

[37] Stehlin, *The Prayer Rule of the Theotokos as Prayed by Saint Seraphim of Sarov*, ix.

[38] Ibid., 1.

[39] Ibid., 2.

[40] Ibid., 3.

4. "Lord, have mercy. Lord, have mercy. Lord, have mercy.
Glory to the Father, and to the Son, and to the Holy Spirit,
Now and ever and forever. Amen.
(The Our Father): Our Father, Who art
                          in heaven, hallowed be Thy Name.
Thy Kingdom come, Thy will be done on earth as it is in
Heaven. Give us this day our daily bread, and forgive us
Our trespasses as we forgive those who trespass against
Us. And lead us not into temptation, but deliver us from
The evil one.
For thine is the kingdom and the power and the glory,
Father, Son, and Holy Spirit, now and ever
                                    and forever. Amen.
Lord, have mercy. Lord, have mercy. Lord, have mercy.
Glory to the Father, and to the Son, and to the Holy Spirit,
Now and ever and forever. Amen.
Come, let us adore the King our God!
Come, let us adore Christ, the King and our God!
Come, let us adore and bow down to the only
Lord Jesus Christ, the King and our God!"[41]

5. (The Creed): "I believe in one God, the Father Almighty,
                                Creator of heaven
And earth, of all things visible and invisible.
                                And in one Lord
Jesus Christ, Son of God, the only-begotten, born of the
Father before all ages; Light from Light,
                                true God from true

---

[41] Ibid., 4-5.

God, begotten, not made, one in essence with the Father,
Through Whom all things were made. For us and for our
Salvation He Came down from heaven and was incarnate of
The Holy Spirit and the Virgin Mary
and became man. He was
Crucified for us under Pontius Pilate,
and suffered and was
Buried. He rose on the third day,
according to the Scriptures.
He ascended into heaven and is seated at the right hand
Of the Father. And He is coming again in glory to judge
The living and the dead and His kingdom will have
No end. And in the Holy Spirit, the Lord, the Creator
Of life, Who proceeds from the Father, Who together
With the Father and the Son is worshipped and glorified,
Who spoke through the prophets. In one, holy, catholic,
And apostolic Church. I profess one baptism for the
Remission of sins. I expect the resurrection of the dead,
And the life of the world to come. Amen."[42]

6. "O Lord, open my lips, and my mouth shall
Proclaim Your praise."[43]

After the preliminary prayers are recited, we are called to remember fifteen key events in the life, death, and afterlife of the Blessed Virgin Mary:
"Nativity of the Theotokos…

---

[42] Ibid., 6-7.

[43] Ibid., 8.

"Presentation of the Blessed Virgin and Theotokos...

"Annunciation of the Blessed Theotokos...

"Meeting of the Blessed Virgin with the Righteous Elizabeth...

"Nativity of Christ...

"Purification of the Lord...

"The Flight of the Theotokos with the God-Child into Egypt...

"The Disappearance of the Twelve-Year-Old Boy Jesus in Jerusalem...

"The Miracle Performed at the Wedding in Cana of Galilee...

"The Theotokos Standing at the Cross of the Lord...

"The Resurrection of Christ...

"The Ascension of Christ...

"The Descent of the Holy Spirit on the Apostles and the Theotokos...

"The Dormition of the Blessed Theotokos...

"The Glory of the Theotokos."[44]

Each of the fifteen mysteries is connected to a special prayer request. One of the spiritual children of Bishop Seraphim Zvezdinsky recorded these fifteen designations:

"First decade: Let us remember the birth of the Mother of God – pray for mothers, fathers and children.

"Second decade: Let us remember the Feast of the Presentation of the Blessed Virgin and Mother of God – let

---

[44] Ibid., 11-39.

us pray for those who have lost their way and fallen away from the church.

"Third decade: Let us remember the Annunciation of the Blessed Mother of God – let us pray for the soothing of sorrows and the consolation of those who grieve.

"Fourth decade: Let us remember the meeting of the Blessed Virgin with the righteous Elizabeth – let us pray for the reunion of the separated, for those whose dear ones or children are living away from them or missing.

"Fifth decade: Let us remember the Birth of Christ – let us pray for the rebirth of souls, for new life in Christ.

"Sixth decade: Let us remember the Feast of the Purification of the Lord, and the words uttered by St Simon: 'Yea, a sword shall pierce through thy own soul also' (Luke 2:35). Let us pray that the Mother of God will meet our souls at the hour of our death, and will contrive that we receive the Holy Sacrament with our last breath, and will lead our souls through the terrible torments.

"Seventh decade: Let us remember the flight of the Mother of God with the God-child into Egypt. Let us pray that the Mother of God will help us avoid temptation in this life and deliver us from misfortunes.

"Eighth decade: Let us remember the disappearance of the twelve-year-old boy Jesus in Jerusalem and the sorrow of the Mother of God on this account. Let us pray, begging the Mother of God for the constant repetition of the Jesus Prayer.

"Ninth decade: Let us remember the miracle performed in Cana of Galilee, when the Lord turned water into wine at the words of the Mother of God: 'They have no wine' (John 2.3). Let us ask the Mother of God for help in our affairs and deliverance from need.

"Tenth decade: Let us remember the Mother of God standing at the cross of the Lord, when grief pierced through her heart like a sword. Let us pray to the Mother of God for the strengthening of our souls for the banishment of despondency.

"Eleventh decade: Let us remember the Resurrection of Christ and ask the Mother of God in prayer to resurrect our souls and give us a new courage for spiritual feats.

"Twelfth decade: Let us remember the Ascension of Christ, at which the Mother of God was present. Let us pray and ask the Queen of Heaven to raise up our souls from earthly and worldly amusement and direct them to striving for higher things.

"Thirteenth decade: Let us remember the Upper Room and the descent of the Holy Spirit on the Apostles and the Mother of God. Let us pray: 'Create in me a clean heart, O God; and renew a right spirit within me. Cast me not away from thy presence; and take not thy holy spirit from me' (Psalm 51.10-11 EB).

"Fourteenth decade: Let us remember the Assumption of the Blessed Mother of God, and ask for a peaceful and serene end.

"Fifteenth decade: Let us remember the glory of the Mother of God, with which the Lord crowned her after her removal from earth to heaven, and let us pray to the Queen of Heaven not to abandon the faithful who are on earth but to defend them from every evil, covering them with her honourable protecting veil."[45]

After each mystery and its accompanying prayer request are recalled, the "Rejoice, O Virgin Theotokos" prayer is repeated ten times. After this, within each mystery, the help of "Our Lady, Blessed Theotokos" is invoked for each of the fifteen special prayer requests, and the "Our Father" is prayed. Finally, each of the fifteen decades closes with the prayer to Our Lady begun with the invocation, "Open unto us the door of your loving-kindness, O blessed Theotokos."[46]

After the preparatory prayers and the fifteen decades are recited, *The Prayer Rule of the Theotokos* concludes with the following:

> "It is truly proper to glorify you, O Theotokos, the
> Ever blessed, immaculate and the Mother of God.
> More honorable than the Cherubim and beyond compare
> More glorious than the Seraphim, who a Virgin gave
> Birth to God the Word, you, truly the Theotokos,
> We magnify.
> Glory to the Father, and to the Son, and to the Holy Spirit,
> Now and ever and forever. Amen.
> Lord, have mercy. Lord, have mercy. Lord, have mercy.
> Through the prayers of
>   thy Most Holy Mother, the Theotokos
> And Ever-Virgin Mary, and through

---

[45] Ibid., 67-69.
[46] Ibid., iv, vi, viii, 11-39.

the prayers of our holy fathers,
And of all the saints, O Lord Jesus Christ our God,
Have mercy on us. Amen."[47]

---

[47] Ibid., 41.

THE ROSARY

"Hail Mary, full of grace. The Lord is with thee. Blessed art thou among women, and blessed is the fruit of thy womb, Jesus. Holy Mary, Mother of God, pray for us sinners, now and at the hour of our death. Amen."[48]

"St. Augustine calls Mary the living 'mold of God,' and that indeed she is; for it was in her alone that God was made a true man without losing any feature of the Godhead, and it is also in her alone that man can be truly formed into God, in so far as that is possible for human nature, by the grace of Jesus Christ."[49] Prayers to Our Lady accompanied this pious devotion with the purpose of deepening and enhancing our love for Jesus. "He who is cast in this mold is presently formed and molded in Jesus Christ, and Jesus Christ in him."[50] The Rosary developed throughout history to help fulfill this Christological challenge. "The Rosary is like a mighty stream whose waters are drawn from many tributaries. They all have

---

[48] Kasten, *Linking Your Beads: The Rosary's History, Mysteries, and Prayers*, 52-53.

[49] St. Louis de Montfort, *The Secret of Mary* (Charlotte, NC: TAN Books, 1998), 14-15.

[50] St. Louis de Montfort, *True Devotion to Mary* (Charlotte, NC: TAN Books, 2010), 120.

their source in the same spiritual heights – the liturgical prayers of the Church, not as directed to the celebration of the Holy Mass, but as establishing a prayerful relationship to God."[51]

The Rosary with its mysteries helps us fix our hearts and minds upon the life, death, and resurrection of Jesus Christ. Priests called to preach from the pulpit may point their people to the mysteries of the Rosary. "We ought to emulate Saint Paul who knew and preached nothing but Jesus Crucified. This is really and truly what you will be doing if you preach the Holy Rosary. It is not just a conglomeration of Our Fathers and Hail Marys, but on the contrary it is a divine summary of the mysteries of the life, Passion, death and glory of Jesus and Mary."[52] The Rosary offers the opportunity to strive for union and communion with God through Jesus Christ His Son and Mary the Mother of God.

The Rosary contains unique and particular physical characteristics. "It is a circular string or chain of beads composed of five decades of small beads separated by five larger beads with a pendant attached, consisting of a cross or crucifix, and a chain or two large and three smaller beads. This device is used to count the prayers recited in honour of the Blessed Virgin Mary while meditating on scenes from the life of Christ and His Mother. A complete 'rosary' requires three repetitions of this chaplet, covering

---

[51] Franz Michel William, *The Rosary: Its History and Meaning* (New York: Christ the King Library, 1952), 11.

[52] St. Louis de Montfort, *The Secret of the Rosary* (Charlotte, NC: TAN Books, 1993), 11.

the full fifteen 'mysteries of salvation'. Pope Pius XII called it 'the compendium of the entire Gospel.'"[53]

"For 400 years or more it was generally accepted that the rosary as a Marian prayer was given by the Blessed Virgin to St Dominic in a dream to assist him in his effort to convert the Cathars."[54] Actually, the thought of Saint Dominic as the primary proponent of the Rosary did not develop until close to 250 years after his death. "The linkage between the rosary and St Dominic would seem to have been proposed by Alain de la Roche, a Dominican friar and founder of the first rosary confraternity in 1468-70."[55] Modern scholarship sees the development of the Rosary as springing from a gradual process of development rather than from the dream of Saint Dominic. "A full review of the rosary will show that there was no one point of origin, rather it evolved over a long period and from a variety of sources."[56]

The use of prayer knots or beads seems deep-rooted and ingrained in the consciousness of people praying to God from the earliest days of human history. "Thus it was the custom of the hermits of the Orient, as far back as the fourth century, to devise a sequence of certain prayers, which they counted on pebbles."[57] A similar se-

---

[53] John D. Miller, *Beads & Prayers: The Rosary in History & Devotion* (London: Burns and Oates, 2002), 1.

[54] Ibid., 7.

[55] Ibid., 11.

[56] Ibid.

[57] Paul A. Böer, Sr., *Enchiridion Sanctissimi Rosarii: A Manual of the Most Holy Rosary* (Dublin: Veritatis Splendor Publications,

quencing using spiritual roses in a wreath honored Our Lady during this time. "St. Gregory, at the end of the fourth century, spoke of such a method of devotion in veneration of the Blessed Virgin Mary. This pious bishop thought a wreath of spiritual roses would be more pleasing to the blessed Virgin than the natural roses with which the faithful adorned her altar. He selected, therefore, a number of prayers, in praise of the blessed Virgin, and united them in a wreath. And this was the origin of the rosary, woven by pious hands for the veneration of Mary, the mystical rose."[58]

The veneration of Mary continued unabated. "The Angelic Salutation and Elizabeth's greeting of Mary are found in the Eastern Liturgy from perhaps the fifth century."[59] In addition, a fifth century legend asserts that "St. Brigid urgently commended the devotion of the rosary, and she chose as its prayers the Our Father, the Hail Mary, and the Creed, and united them into a wreath of prayers. In order to count their recital she strung little beads of stone or wood and made a wreath of them."[60]

Devotion to Mary took many forms in early church history. The transition to the modern Rosary began in earnest by linking it to the recitation of the 150 Psalms in the Divine Office.

2013), 19.

[58] Ibid., 20.

[59] Miller, *Beads & Prayers: The Rosary in History & Devotion*, 12.

[60] Böer, *Enchiridion Sanctissimi Rosarii: A Manual of the Most Holy Rosary*, 20.

"From time immemorial the 150 Psalms of the Bible have comprised the most important part of the canonical hours."[61] With the vast majority of the laity being illiterate and unable to read the Psalms, attempts were made to allow them to pray with a similar point of reference. Analogous to the established reciting of the 150 Psalms, church leaders offered to the laity in various ways "another series of prayers composed of 150 individual parts. Here we have the beginnings of the rosary."[62]

A further movement in the development of the Rosary occurred in Ireland. The Irish monks "had a special name for the Psalter. The 150 Psalms were the *Na tri coicat*, which meant 'the three fifties.' Here, at two places in this isle of saints, we have the beginnings of our prayer. Its final and complete development is our present-day rosary."[63]

One instance of prayer dedicated to praying with the three sets of fifty occurred in the life of Saint Patrick, the patron saint and fifth century bishop of Ireland. "It is related of the Saint that he divided the night into three parts: the first two devoted to prayer, the last third to sleep. He spent the time allotted to prayer in such wise as to recite one hundred Psalms, or two 'fifties,' and to make two hundred genuflection, one at the beginning and one at the end of each Psalm. The last 'fifty' he prayed while standing in

---

[61] William, *The Rosary: Its History and Meaning*, 11.
[62] Ibid., 12.
[63] Ibid., 13.

cold water, with arms extended, in order to keep himself awake and to do penance."[64]

Because the laity could not read the Psalter, they eventually were encouraged to pray 150 Our Fathers in lieu of the 150 Psalms. "All the way back in the ninth century, monks were encouraging laymen who could not read to recite a series of 'Our Fathers' in place of the daily office and Breviary in which they were unable to participate. It became popular to use 150 'Our Fathers' because of the 150 psalms in the Psalter."[65] As devotion to the Blessed Virgin Mary continued, people began praying 150 Hail Marys instead of 150 Our Fathers. "In the course of time another psalter came to be associated with the psalter of the 150 Our Fathers. It consisted of 150 Hail Marys in the formula then current."[66]

The earliest form of the Hail Mary consisted in two biblical quotations from the Gospel of Luke. The angel Gabriel greets the Theotokos with these words: "Hail, thou that art highly favored, the Lord [is] with thee."[67] The evangelist Luke records this event in his gospel, and the detailed description of Mary's conversation with the angel is precise and powerful. "Especially when it is a question of events as intimate as the virginal conception,

---

[64] Ibid., 16.

[65] Rev. Edward Hughes, *Paraliturgical Devotions of the Western Church and Their Role in Orthodoxy* (Stanton, NJ: Saint Luke's Priory Press, 1992), 5.

[66] William, *The Rosary: Its History and Meaning*, 18.

[67] Luke 1.28 (ASV).

the source could have been only Mary herself."[68] Similarly, in another personal encounter, Elizabeth greets the Virgin Mary with this proclamation: "Blessed art thou among women, and blessed is the fruit of thy womb."[69] There are several liturgical references to the twin greetings. "The union of the two greetings, that of the Angel and that of Elizabeth, in one formula is found in the Liturgies of St James of Antioch and St Mark of Alexandria, which may go back to the fifth, or even fourth, century."[70] In addition, "an Egyptian ostracon dated about AD 600… bears in Greek the following inscription: Hail Mary, full of grace, the Lord is with thee, blessed art thou amongst women, and blessed is the fruit of thy womb, because you have conceived Christ, the Son of God, redeemer of our souls."[71] This special prayer also is found in the West. "In the Western liturgy, this prayer formula is assigned from the seventh century as an offertory antiphon for the Feast of the Annunciation, the Ember Wednesday of Advent, and the fourth Sunday in Advent in the Antiphonary traditionally attributed to St Gregory the Great."[72]

The first part of the prayer, "Hail Mary, full of grace, the Lord is with thee," was featured prominently in the Saturday

---

[68] Lucien Deiss, *Joseph, Mary, Jesus* (Collegeville, MN: Liturgical Press, 1996), 37.

[69] Luke 1.42 (KJV).

[70] Miller, *Beads & Prayers: The Rosary in History & Devotion*, 39.

[71] Ibid.

[72] Ibid., 40.

Office honoring the Blessed Virgin Mary.[73] The second part, "blessed art thou among women, and blessed is the fruit of thy womb," was used as an Antiphon at Vespers and Lauds.[74] "From the thirteenth century the Hail Mary was a favorite prayer of the faithful. They put it on a par with the Creed and the Our Father and prayed it with them."[75] "The addition of the word '*Jesus*' or '*Jesus Christus. Amen*', dates from the thirteenth century, and the final invocation to Mary was added towards the end of the fifteenth century. The current form was fixed in the sixteenth century."[76]

The Rosary involves more than the simple recitation of prayers. "The most distinctive feature of the devotion today is its combination of oral repetition with serial mental meditations."[77] The praying of the Rosary corresponds to the Divine Office and the praying of the Psalms. "The complete Rosary contains 15 decades of Aves—150 Hail Marys corresponding to 150 Psalms."[78] While pronouncing the prayers, the faithful meditate on the life, death, and resurrection of Jesus Christ. "The 150 Aves—divided into three sets of fifty—are recited orally in groups of ten punctuated by an Our Father. During each set of ten Aves

---

[73] William, *The Rosary: Its History and Meaning*, 20.

[74] Ibid.

[75] Ibid., 22.

[76] Miller, *Beads & Prayers: The Rosary in History & Devotion*, 53.

[77] Anne Winston-Allen, *Stories of the Rose: The Making of the Rosary in the Middle Ages* (University Park, PA: Penn State University Press, 1997), 3.

[78] Böer, *Enchiridion Sanctissimi Rosarii: A Manual of the Most Holy Rosary*, 93.

the worshiper meditates on one of a series of fifteen mysteries, events in the life of Christ and Mary that comprise five joyful, five sorrowful, and five glorious episodes."[79]

The Rosary begins with the Sign of the Cross.[80] The special beads and particular prayers of a five-decade Rosary follow this pious path:

1. The Crucifix: The Creed
2. The Pater Bead: The Our Father
3. The Three Ave Beads: Three Hail Marys
4. The Gloria Bead: The Glory Be
5. The First Decade: The Our Father on the Pater Bead, Ten Hail Marys on the Ave Beads, The Glory Be on the Gloria Bead
6. The Second Decade: The Our Father on the Pater Bead, Ten Hail Marys on the Ave Beads, The Glory Be on the Gloria Bead
7. The Third Decade: The Our Father on the Pater Bead, Ten Hail Marys on the Ave Beads, The Glory Be on the Gloria Bead
8. The Fourth Decade: The Our Father on the Pater Bead, Ten Hail Marys on the Ave Beads, The Glory Be on the Gloria Bead
9. The Fifth Decade: The Our Father on the Pater Bead, Ten Hail Marys on the Ave Beads, The Glory Be on the Gloria Bead[81]

---

[79] Winston-Allen, *Stories of the Rose: The Making of the Rosary in the Middle Ages*, 3.

[80] Böer, *Enchiridion Sanctissimi Rosarii: A Manual of the Most Holy Rosary*, 91.

[81] Ibid., 92-97.

10. The Hail Holy Queen: "Hail holy Queen, mother of mercy, our life, our sweetness, and our hope. To thee do we cry, poor banished children of Eve. To thee do we send up our sighs, mourning and weeping in this valley of tears. Turn then, most gracious Advocate, thine eyes of mercy toward us. And after this our exile show unto us the blessed Fruit of thy womb, Jesus. O clement, O loving, O sweet Virgin Mary. Amen."[82]

"Traditionally the Rosary consists of three sets of mysteries, the Joyful, Sorrowful, and Glorious. However in October 2002, Pope John Paul II proposed five additional mysteries to the Rosary in his Apostolic Letter *Rosarium Virginis Mariae*. The Luminous Mysteries or Mysteries of Light provide opportunity for us to meditate on the public ministry of Jesus, those years between His childhood and His Passion. The pope made it clear that these were optional for the faithful. But since their proposal, they have become regularly used by the faithful."[83] The traditional fifteen Joyful, Sorrowful, and Glorious Mysteries and the newly-developed five Luminous Mysteries each constitute a decade of the Rosary, with an Our Father, ten Hail Marys, and the Glory Be:

1. "The Joyful Mysteries: The Childhood of Christ
2. "The Annunciation of the Angel St. Gabriel to the Blessed Virgin

---

[82] Ibid., 111.
[83] Ibid., 98.

3. "The Visitation of the Blessed Virgin to St. Elizabeth
4. "The Nativity of Our Lord Jesus Christ
5. "The Presentation of Our Lord in the Temple
6. "The Finding of Our Lord in the Temple
7. "The Luminous Mysteries: The Public Life of Christ
8. "The Baptism of Our Lord
9. "Wedding at Cana
10. "The Proclamation of the Kingdom of God
11. "The Transfiguration of Christ
12. "The Institution of the Eucharist
13. "The Sorrowful Mysteries: The Passion of Christ
14. "The Agony of Our Lord in the Garden
15. "The Scourging of Our Lord at the Pillar
16. "The Crowning with Thorns
17. "The Carrying of the Cross
18. "The Death of Our Savior on the Cross
19. "The Glorious Mysteries: The Resurrection of Christ
20. "The Resurrection of Our Lord
21. "The Ascension of Our Lord into Heaven
22. "The Coming of the Holy Ghost at Pentecost
23. "The Assumption of the Blessed Virgin, Body and Soul, into Heaven
24. "The Coronation of the Blessed Virgin in Heaven by Our Lord"[84]

---

[84] Ibid., 93-110.

THEOLOGICAL REFLECTION

"If God were going to become man to be born on earth as we are, He would have to choose an exceptional woman to be His mother on earth. This woman would have to be pure, holy and full of faith. She would have to be consecrated and guided from her childhood for this great service."[85] Unlike the Rosary, *The Prayer Rule of the Theotokos* adds two mysteries involving the early years of Mary's life: The Nativity of the Theotokos and the Presentation of the Blessed Virgin Mary at the Temple.

The Nativity of the Theotokos features prominently in the Orthodox Church. "The chaste Joachim departed to the wilderness and dwelt there, fasting and offering up prayer to God that he might become a father."[86] Despite being apart, Anna joined her prayers to those of her husband. "Meanwhile, the like-minded Anna shut herself in a nearby garden and cried to the Lord with pain in her heart, 'Hear me, O God of my fathers, and bless me, as you blessed Sarah's womb.' And the Lord heard them and bless-

---

[85] Archbishop Lazar Puhalo, *The Most Holy Theotokos* (Dewdney, Canada: Synaxis Press, 1999), 3.

[86] St. Gregory Palamas, *Mary the Mother of God: Sermons by Saint Gregory Palamas*, ed. Christopher Veniamin (South Caanan, PA: Mount Thabor Publishing, 2005), 3.

ed them, and promised to give them a child."[87] *The Prayer Rule of the Theotokos* recognizes the eternal relevance of the birth of the Blessed Virgin Mary by making her Nativity the first great mystery. "Now He has fulfilled this promise and has granted them a daughter more wonderful than all the wonders down through the ages, the Mother of the Creator of the universe, who made the human race divine, turned earth into heaven, made God into the Son of man, and men into the sons of God."[88]

The second profound mystery in *The Prayer Rule of the Theotokos* and absent in the Rosary is the Presentation of the Theotokos in the Temple. At the age of three, Mary entered the temple of the Lord.[89] "Today, she is about to be welcomed by the sanctity of the Spirit into the holy of holies; she, who was raised in a most marvelous way beyond even the glory of the cherubim, is stored up in a most holy way and gloriously in the holy of holies, for a greater sanctity, at an innocent and impressionable age."[90] The High Priest welcomed the Virgin Mary into the temple. "Immediately leaving everyone behind, her parents, nurses and contemporaries, she separated herself from the assembled company and went forward to the High Priest,

---

[87] Ibid., 4.

[88] Ibid.

[89] Frederica Mathewes-Green, *The Lost Gospel of Mary: The Mother of Jesus in Three Ancient Texts* (Brewster, MA: Paraclete Press, 2007), 43.

[90] Mary B. Cunningham, trans., *Wider Than Heaven: Eighth-century Homilies on the Mother of God* (Crestwood, NY: St. Vladimir's Seminary Press, 2008), 147.

absolutely alone and full of joy."[91] Undoubtedly filled with joy and wonder, "the priest welcomed Mary and kissed her, and blessed her saying, 'The Lord has magnified your name to all generations of the earth. By you, unto the last of days, the Lord God will reveal redemption to the children of Israel.' Then he sat her down on the third step of the altar, and the Lord God poured out grace upon her. And she danced with her feet, and all the house of Israel loved her."[92] Mary's status of the Mother of God is unparalleled in all of human history. "She alone dwelt in the Holy of Holies… Neither before nor after her had there appeared a virgin mother or a mother of God, and no one before or after her had dwelt in the Holy of Holies."[93]

The addition of these two great mysteries in *The Prayer Rule of the Theotokos* right at the beginning distinguishes it from the Rosary. The next six mysteries in *The Prayer Rule of the Theotokos* include all the Five Joyful Mysteries of the Rosary, the Annunciation, the Visitation, the Nativity of Jesus, the Presentation, and the Finding of Jesus in the Temple at the age of twelve, while adding the Flight of the Theotokos with the God-Child into Egypt. The first public miracle of Jesus during the Wedding Feast at Cana is the ninth mystery in *The Prayer Rule of the Theotokos* and features prominently as the first of five Luminous Mysteries

---

[91] Palamas, *Mary the Mother of God: Sermons by Saint Gregory Palamas*, 12.

[92] Mathewes-Green, *The Lost Gospel of Mary: The Mother of Jesus in Three Ancient Texts*, 43.

[93] Palamas, *Mary the Mother of God: Sermons by Saint Gregory Palamas*, 4.

in the Rosary. Ignoring the rest of the Luminous Mysteries and all of the Sorrowful Mysteries in the Rosary, *The Prayer Rule of the Theotokos* presents one poignant picture of the Passion of Christ, the Theotokos standing at the Cross of Christ as its tenth mystery. The last five mysteries of *The Prayer Rule of the Theotokos* mirror the Five Glorious Mysteries of the Rosary with several slight variations in wording. Although the Resurrection and the Ascension are the same, *The Prayer Rule of the Theotokos* emphasizes in its prayer that the Theotokos was present at both the Ascension and the Descent of the Holy Ghost at Pentecost. In addition, whereas *The Prayer Rule of the Theotokos* speaks of the Dormition of the Theotokos, the Rosary presents the Assumption of Mary. Finally, both *The Prayer Rule of the Theotokos* and the Rosary focus upon the Glory of the Theotokos as the Lord Jesus crowns her as the Queen of Heaven. The mysteries of *The Prayer Rule of the Theotokos* and the Rosary contain many similarities with some significant differences.

The actual format of *The Prayer Rule of the Theotokos* and the Rosary also contains some similarities and differences. The introduction of both prayers begins with the Sign of the Cross and features the Creed, the Our Father, and the Glory Be. In addition, the traditional rendition of the Rosary features fifteen decades as does *The Prayer Rule of the Theotokos*, with the Rosary recently adding the optional Luminous Mysteries. For each decade, an Our Father and ten prayers containing the Angelic and Elizabethan greetings from the Gospel of Luke are included, although the rest of the prayer differs in substance. In this regard, the central recitation in *The Prayer Rule of the Theotokos* declares, "Rejoice, O Virgin Theotokos Mary, full of grace, the Lord is with You. Blessed are you among women, and blessed is the fruit of Your womb, for you have born Christ, the Savior of our souls."[94] Similarly, the pivotal prayer to Our Lady in the Rosary differs slightly and is spoken, "Hail Mary, full of grace. The Lord is with thee. Blessed art thou among women, and blessed is the fruit of thy womb, Jesus. Holy Mary, Mother of God, pray for us sinners, now and at the hour of our death. Amen."[95] Calling the Blessed Virgin Mary by her name is biblical; the faithful calling her the Theotokos "early in the fourth century and very possibly a century before that"[96] magnifies her unique prominence within church tradition. Using both titles by memorizing and praying both prayers rather than only one deepens our understanding and appreciation of this uniqueness. "She is truly the God-bearer, and through her all creation has received, by God's saving plan, the great gift of the presence in the flesh of the only Son and Word of God the Father."[97]

---

[94] Stehlin, *The Prayer Rule of the Theotokos as Prayed by Saint Seraphim of Sarov*, iv.

[95] Kasten, *Linking Your Beads: The Rosary's History, Mysteries, and Prayers*, 52-53.

[96] Richard M. Price, "The *Theotokos* and the Council of Ephesus," Chap. 6 in *The Origins of the Cult of the Virgin Mary*, ed. Chris Maunder (London: Burns and Oates, 2008), 90.

[97] Brian E. Daley, *On the Dormition of Mary* (Crestwood, NY: St. Vladimir's Seminary Press, 1997), 47.

Either of these prayers, repeated often with great devotion and veneration, nurtures our relationship with the Theotokos and deepens our love for her Son Jesus. The centerpiece of both *The Prayer Rule of the Theotokos* and the Rosary is the prayer to Our Lady. The repetition of these prayers undoubtedly brings great joy to the Mother of God. "This angelic salutation is most pleasing to the ever-blessed Virgin; for whenever she hears it, it would seem as if the joy which she experienced when St. Gabriel announced to her that she was the chosen Mother of God, was renewed in her; and with this object in view, we should often salute her with the 'Hail Mary.'"[98]

Clearly "the Mother's virginity serves as a 'sign' of the Son's uniqueness."[99] Our love for the Theotokos reveals a deeper understanding of the dual nature of Jesus Christ, fully God and fully man. "His birth from a virgin emphasizes that, while immanent, he is also transcendent; although completely man, he is also perfect God."[100] Both *The Prayer Rule of the Theotokos* and the Rosary point to the life, death, and resurrection of Jesus Christ as seen through the eyes of the Blessed Virgin Mary.

Simeon the prophet warned Mary that "a sword shall pierce through thy own soul."[101] This prophecy reached fruition during the Passion of Jesus Christ. Saint Max-

---

[98] St. Alphonsus de Liguori, *The Glories of Mary* (Brooklyn, NY: Redemptorist Fathers, 1931), 593.

[99] Bishop Kallistos Ware, *The Orthodox Way* (Crestwood, NY: St. Vladimir's Seminary Press, 1979), 76.

[100] Ibid.

[101] Luke 2:35 KJV.

imus the Confessor describes the depth of Mary's pain and suffering: "When the time of the life-giving Passion arrived, when the gracious and sweet Lord was judged by the high priests and princes and was tortured and crucified, not only was the immaculate mother inseparable from him, but she shared his pain. And I would say, even though it is a bold statement, that she suffered more than him and endured sorrows of the heart: for he was God and Lord of all things, and he willingly endured suffering in the flesh. But she possessed the frailty of a human being and a woman and was filled with such love toward her beloved and desirable son."[102]

The monks and nuns throughout the centuries nurtured a profound love for Our Lady. "Love, devotion and emotions surrounded Mary within the monastic milieu, and radiated out from it."[103] Within the Roman Catholic tradition, the Cistercian Saint Bernard of Clairvaux "was the chief force behind the spiritual revival of the twelfth century as well as being one of the most illustrious statesmen of the time."[104] Within the Cistercians, Saint Bernard's love of Our Lady was beyond compare. "No Cistercian came to be as closely associated with devotion to Mary as St Bernard of Clairvaux."[105] His poem

---

[102] Maximus the Confessor, *The Life of the Virgin*, trans. Stephen J. Shoemaker (New Haven and London: Yale University Press, 2012), 101.

[103] Rubin, *Mother of God: A History of the Virgin Mary*, 149.

[104] Thomas Bokenkotter, *A Concise History of the Catholic Church* (New York and London: Doubleday, 2004), 148.

[105] Rubin, *Mother of God: A History of the Virgin Mary*, 150.

dedicated to the Blessed Virgin Mary offers veneration and inspiration:

> Our Lady,
> Our mediatrix,
> Our advocate,
> To your Son, reconcile us,
> To your Son, commend us,
> To your Son, present us.
> Obtain,
> O blessed lady,
> By the grace found in you,
> By the privilege deserved by you,
> By the mercy born of you,
> That he who,
> By your mediation,
> Deigned to share our infirmity
> And our misery,
> May, by your intercession,
> Let us also share his glory
> And his blessedness,
> He, Jesus Christ,
> Your Son,
> Our Lord,
> Blessed above all
> For ever and ever.[106]

---

[106] Ibid. 12.

CONCLUSION

"From apostolic times and to our days all who truly love Christ give veneration to Her Who gave birth to Him, raised Him and protected Him in the days of His youth. If God the Father chose Her, God the Holy Spirit descended upon Her, and God the Son dwelt in Her, submitted to Her in the days of His youth, was concerned for Her when hanging on the Cross—then should not everyone who confess the Holy Trinity venerate Her?"[107]

According to one Orthodox scholar, "the Rosary itself contains nothing contrary to Orthodoxy either in doctrine or in spirit."[108] Stated in the affirmative, the Western Rosary "is a laudable mediation on the Incarnation and lives of Christ and Mary. All but the last two of the mysteries are taken directly from Biblical texts. One need only look at the liturgical texts of the east to substantiate that these also are part of the Orthodox tradition."[109] This scholar's point is excellent, and I would go a step further, inviting and encouraging Orthodox

---

[107] St. John Maximovitch, *The Orthodox Veneration of the Mother of God* (Platina, CA: St. Herman of Alaska Brotherhood, 2012), 21.

[108] Hughes, *Paraliturgical Devotions of the Western Church and Their Role in Orthodoxy*, 8.

[109] Ibid., 7.

Christians, both East and West, to pray both *The Prayer Rule of the Theotokos* and the Rosary, thus exploring more in depth the richness and diversity within our one tradition.

"True devotion to Our Lady is interior; that is, it comes from the mind and the heart. It flows from the esteem we have for her, the high idea we have formed of her greatness, and the love which we have for her."[110] The more we pray to the Blessed Virgin Mary, the deeper our intimacy with her Son Jesus, conceived by the Holy Spirit, born from her womb, nurtured from her breast as a child, and lovingly embraced by her upon His death on the cross. Father Arseny, a priest imprisoned in the Soviet Union, describes the deliverance from a frightening experience bringing the loving relationship between Jesus and His Mother to light: "The eyes of the Mother of God looked at me from the icon. Her face was bent toward her child, who pressed His cheek tightly against hers. In this embrace you could see the unbelievable love and desire of the Mother to protect her child, to warm him with her love, the love only a mother can give."[111] By praying both *The Prayer Rule of the Theotokos* and the Rosary from deep within our interior hearts and minds, we draw closer to Jesus and His Mother.

Mary is our Mother. Whatever your station in life, her virtuous life as one chosen by God and pursuing a

---

[110] Montfort, *True Devotion to Mary*, 54.

[111] Vera Bouteneff, trans., *Father Arseny, 1893-1973: Priest, Prisoner, Spiritual Father* (Crestwood, NY: St. Vladimir's Seminary Press, 1998), 226.

life of holiness inspires each of us to love both her and her Son Jesus. As the Virgin Mother of God, perhaps her finest and most unique virtue is purity. "Blessed are the pure in heart, for they shall see God."[112] Deepening our relationship with Jesus Christ by faithfully praying *The Prayer Rule of the Theotokos* and the Rosary purifies our hearts and helps us address whatever separates us from God. "The problem of purity arises in every age of human life, from early infancy to last old age, and in every condition of life."[113] The Blessed Virgin Mary can assist us in our daily battle to live pure and holy lives.

Roman Catholic priest and poet Gerard Manley Hopkins invites us to love the Blessed Virgin Mary and immerse ourselves in this purity and holiness:

> Be thou then, O thou dear
> Mother, my atmosphere;
> My happier world, wherein
> To wend and meet no sin;
> Above me, round me lie
> Fronting my forward eye
> With sweet and scarless sky;
> Stir in my eyes, speak there
> Of God's love, O live air,
> Of patience, penance, prayer:

---

[112] Matthew 5.8 (NASB).

[113] Jean Guitton, *The Blessed Virgin* (London: Burns and Oates, 1952), 17.

World-mothering air, air wild,
Wound with thee, in thee isled,
Fold home, fast fold thy child.[114]

---

[114] Gerard Manley Hopkins, "The Blessed Virgin compared to the Air we Breathe," lines 114-126.

BIBLIOGRAPHY

Athans, Mary Christine. *In Quest of the Jewish Mary*. Maryknoll, NY: Orbis Books, 2013.

Böer, Sr., Paul A. *Enchiridion Sanctissimi Rosarii: A Manual of the Most Holy Rosary*. Dublin: Veritatis Splendor Publications, 2013.

Bokenkotter, Thomas. *A Concise History of the Catholic Church*. New York and London: Doubleday, 2004.

Bouteneff, Vera, trans. *Father Arseny, 1893-1973: Priest, Prisoner, Spiritual Father*. Crestwood, NY: St. Vladimir's Seminary Press, 1998.

Bulgakov, Sergius. *The Burning Bush: On the Orthodox Veneration of the Mother of God*. Grand Rapids, MI: William B. Eerdsman Publishing, 2009.

Cunningham, Mary B., trans. *Wider Than Heaven: Eighth-century Homilies on the Mother of God*. Crestwood, NY: St. Vladimir's Seminary Press, 2008.

Daley, Brian E. *On the Dormition of Mary*. Crestwood, NY: St. Vladimir's Seminary Press, 1997.

Deiss, Lucien. *Joseph, Mary, Jesus*. Collegeville, MN: Liturgical Press, 1996.

Ellis, Jane, trans. *An Early Soviet Saint: The Life of Father Zachariah*. London and Oxford: Mowbrays, 1976.

Fastiggi, Robert L. "The Immaculate Conception: Historical and Ecumenical Perspectives," in *De Maria Numquam Satis: The Significance of the Catholic Doctrines on the Blessed Virgin Mary*, edited by Judith Marie Gentle and Robert L. Fastiggi, 1-16. Lanham, MD: University Press of America, 2009.

Gambero, Luigi. *Mary and the Fathers of the Church: The Blessed Virgin Mary in Patristic Thought*. San Francisco: Ignatius Press, 1999.

Graef, Hilda. *Mary: A History of Doctrine and Devotion*, vol. 1. New York: Sheed and Ward, 1963.

Guitton, Jean. *The Blessed Virgin*. London: Burns and Oates, 1952.

Holy Transfiguration Monastery, trans. *The Service of the Akathist Hymn: The Salutations to the Most Holy Theotokos*. Boston, MA: Holy Transfiguration Monastery, 1991.

Hughes, Rev. Edward. *Paraliturgical Devotions of the Western Church and Their Role in Orthodoxy.* Stanton, NJ: Saint Luke's Priory Press, 1992.

"I. M. Andreyev: True Orthodox Convert from the Russian Intelligentsia." *The Orthodox Word 73*, 13.2, March-April, 1977.

Jacob of Serug. *On the Mother of God.* Crestwood, NY: St. Vladimir's Seminary Press, 1998.

Kasten, Patricia Ann. *Linking Your Beads: The Rosary's History, Mysteries, and Prayers.* Huntington, IN: Our Sunday Visitor, 2010.

Liguori, St. Alphonsus de. *The Glories of Mary.* Brooklyn, NY: Redemptorist Fathers, 1931.

Louth, Andrew. "John of Damascus on the Mother of God as a Link Between Humanity and God." Chap. 10 in *The Cult of the Mother of God in Byzantium,* edited by Leslie Brubaker and Mary Cunningham, 153-161. Burlington, VT: Ashgate Publishing, 2011.

Mathewes-Green, Frederica. *The Lost Gospel of Mary: The Mother of Jesus in Three Ancient Texts.* Brewster, MA: Paraclete Press, 2007.

Maximovitch, St. John. *The Orthodox Veneration of the Mother of God*. Platina, CA: St. Herman of Alaska Brotherhood, 2012.

Maximus the Confessor. *The Life of the Virgin*, trans. Stephen J. Shoemaker. New Haven and London: Yale University Press, 2012.

McGuckin, John Anthony. *The Harp of Glory: Enzira Sebhat*. Yonkers, NY: St. Vladimir's Seminary Press, 2010.

Miller, John D. *Beads & Prayers: The Rosary in History & Devotion*. London: Burns and Oates, 2002.

Montfort, St. Louis de. *The Secret of Mary*. Charlotte, NC: TAN Books, 1998.

—. *The Secret of the Rosary*. Charlotte, NC: TAN Books, 1993.

—. *True Devotion to Mary*. Charlotte, NC: TAN Books, 2010.

Palamas, St. Gregory. *Mary the Mother of God: Sermons by Saint Gregory Palamas*, ed. Christopher Veniamin. South Caanan, PA: Mount Thabor Publishing, 2005.

Pelikan, Jaroslav. *Mary Through the Centuries*. New Haven and London: Yale University Press, 1996.

Podolak, Andrew Gary. "*Most Holy Theotokos, Save Us.*" Master's thesis, Balamand University, 2015.

Poems of Gerard Manley Hopkins. New York and London: Oxford University Press, 1948.

Price, Richard M. "The *Theotokos* and the Council of Ephesus." Chap. 6 in *The Origins of the Cult of the Virgin Mary,* edited by Chris Maunder, 89-103. London: Burns and Oates, 2008.

Puhalo, Archbishop Lazar. *The Most Holy Theotokos.* Dewdney, Canada: Synaxis Press, 1999.

Reynolds, Brian K. *Gateway to Heaven: Marian Doctrine and Devotion Image and Typology in the Patristic and Medieval Period*, vol. 1. Hyde Park, NY: New City Press, 2012.

Rubin, Miri. *Mother of God: A History of the Virgin Mary.* New Haven & London: Yale University Press, 2009.

Stehlin, Anthony. *The Prayer Rule of the Theotokos as Prayed by Saint Seraphim of Sarov.* Middletown, DE: Chi Rho Publishing, 2015.

Ware, Bishop Kallistos. *The Orthodox Way.* Crestwood, NY: St. Vladimir's Seminary Press, 1979.

Ware, Timothy. *The Orthodox Church.* London: Penguin Books, 1997.

William, Franz Michel. *The Rosary: Its History and Meaning*. New York: Christ the King Library, 1952.

Winston-Allen, Anne. *Stories of the Rose: The Making of the Rosary in the Middle Ages*. University Park, PA: Penn State University Press, 1997.

THE JOY OF ORTHODOXY

DEACON DAVID LOCHBIHLER, J.D.

ORTHODOX LOGOS PUBLISHING

www.ingramcontent.com/pod-product-compliance
Lightning Source LLC
Chambersburg PA
CBHW021133080526
44587CB00012B/1261